TOXIC FAMILY GATHERINGS

What to Say, How to Act, and When to Leave Without Making Things Worse

Disclaimer:

This book is intended for informational and educational purposes only.

The content is based on general principles for navigating difficult interpersonal situations and is not a substitute for professional advice. Nothing in this book should be considered medical, psychological, legal, or therapeutic guidance.

Family dynamics and personal circumstances vary widely. The strategies and examples in this book may not be appropriate for every situation. Readers are responsible for deciding how, when, and whether to apply any suggestions discussed.

If you are experiencing severe emotional distress, abuse, or situations that involve threats to your safety or well-being, professional support from a qualified healthcare provider, counselor, or other appropriate professional is strongly recommended.

The author and publisher make no guarantees regarding outcomes and assume no responsibility for the actions or decisions of the reader.

Dedication

For anyone who has carried emotional baggage into family gatherings.

You're allowed to put it down.

James H.

Table of Contents

Chapter 1
Why This Book Exists (and What It's Not)

F amily gatherings aren't supposed to feel like emotional obstacle courses. And yet for many people, holidays, birthdays, weddings, reunions, and casual "just stop by for dinner" events come with a familiar mix of tension, guilt, awkward comments, old arguments, and the pressure to stay polite no matter what. You may go in with good intentions, only to leave feeling drained, frustrated, or quietly angry at yourself for getting pulled into the same patterns again.

This book exists because that experience is far more common than people admit. It also exists because most advice about it isn't very helpful. You're often told to "just ignore it," "be the bigger person," or "set better boundaries," without anyone explaining what that actually looks like in real time, with real people, in real rooms.

Other advice goes in the opposite direction, pushing deep emotional work or drastic solutions that don't fit the situation you're actually trying to navigate.

This book takes a different approach.

- □ It isn't about fixing your family.
- □ It isn't about cutting people off.
- □ It isn't about therapy, healing your past, or finally getting everyone to understand you.

It's about getting through family gatherings without making things worse. That means knowing what to say when conversations turn critical, invasive, or manipulative. It means knowing how to act when you feel cornered, dismissed, or emotionally provoked. And it means knowing when staying is no longer productive, and how to leave without guilt, drama, or a long explanation.

The focus here is practical. Everything in this book is meant to be usable, often in the moment. You'll find clear language, simple strategies, and straightforward scripts you can adapt to your own situations. There's no requirement to confront anyone, open old wounds, or "have it out" unless you genuinely want to.

Many family dynamics persist not because you're doing something wrong, but because you're walking into emotionally loaded situations without a plan.

When people feel pressured, criticized, or ignored, reactions tend to escalate quickly, even when no one intends for that to happen.

A plan changes that.

It allows you to respond instead of react. It helps you avoid overexplaining, defending yourself, or getting pulled into conversations that never go anywhere. Most importantly, it gives you a way to leave a gathering feeling intact, rather than replaying the event in your head for days afterward.

This book won't promise perfect outcomes.

Some people will still be difficult.
Some situations will still be uncomfortable.

But you don't need everything to go well for the experience to be manageable.

- ☐ You don't need to win arguments.

- ☐ You don't need to explain yourself.

- ☐ You just need a better plan.

That's what this book is here to give you.

How to Use This Book

You don't need to read this book straight through to benefit from it. Some chapters are meant to be skimmed, while others are meant to be revisited before or after a gathering. You may want to read a section the night before an event, refer back to specific scripts during a break, or return to certain chapters afterward to steady your thoughts. Use what applies, skip what doesn't, and come back to it as needed. This book is designed to be a practical tool you can reach for when family dynamics feel difficult, not something that requires deep reflection or perfect follow-through to be helpful.

Chapter 2
Why Family Gatherings Go Sideways (and Why It's Not Just You)

Most difficult family gatherings don't fall apart because someone planned to cause trouble. They unravel because the same unspoken patterns show up every time, and no one pauses them. You walk into the room carrying history. Other people bring expectations, assumptions, old roles, and unfinished conversations. Add time pressure, social obligation, alcohol, or an audience, and even a small comment can land harder than intended. What looks like a random blow-up is usually a predictable sequence.

□ Someone says something familiar.

□ You feel a familiar reaction.

□ You respond the way you always do.

□ And the situation ends the way it usually does.

This chapter is about interrupting that sequence before it runs you over.

The Real Problem Isn't the Comment

When people talk about toxic family dynamics, they often focus on the words.

What was said.

□ How it was said.

□ Who said it.

But the words themselves are rarely the real problem.

The problem is what the comment activates.

- A remark about your job might trigger defensiveness.
- A joke about your relationship might trigger embarrassment.
- A question framed as concern might trigger guilt or anger.

Once that internal reaction kicks in, the conversation is no longer about the topic at hand. It's about protecting yourself, your choices, your boundaries, and your sense of respect. That's when things escalate. The goal of this book is not to stop people from saying irritating things. That's usually out of your control. The goal is to help you recognize when a moment is becoming loaded and respond in a way that keeps you steady rather than reactive.

The Roles You're Expected to Play

Every family has roles, even if no one talks about them.

- The responsible one.
- The peacemaker.
- The one who overreacts.
- The one who gets picked on.
- The one who keeps the peace by staying quiet.

These roles tend to stick, even when people grow up, change careers, build families of their own, or move far away. When everyone gathers again, the old expectations quietly snap back into place. You may notice this the moment you walk through the door.

- You're spoken to differently.
- Your opinions are handled differently.
- Your boundaries are tested in ways they aren't elsewhere.

None of this means you're weak or doing something wrong.It means the environment is primed to pull you into a version of yourself you've outgrown.

Recognizing that is power.

Why "Just Be Yourself" Is Terrible Advice Here

In normal life, authenticity works. In emotionally charged family settings, it can backfire. "Just be yourself" often translates to saying what you feel in the moment, explaining yourself fully, defending your choices, and correcting misunderstandings as they arise.

In a neutral environment, that's reasonable. In a tense family gathering, it often pours fuel on the fire. Not because your feelings are wrong, but because the setting is not designed to receive them well. This book takes a strategic approach instead.

You don't need to show up as your rawest, most vulnerable self in every situation.

You need to show up as the version of yourself who can leave without regret.

The Difference Between Boundaries and Announcements

Many people think setting boundaries means making statements like:

"I'm not going to tolerate this anymore."
"You can't talk to me like that."

"I'm setting a boundary."

Those statements are sometimes necessary.In family gatherings, they often escalate tension quickly. This book focuses on functional boundaries rather than verbal declarations. A functional boundary is something you do, not something you announce.

It might look like changing the subject calmly, giving a brief neutral response instead of an explanation, stepping away from a conversation before it heats up, or leaving earlier than planned without making a point of it. These actions protect your peace without demanding agreement or understanding from anyone else.

The Importance of a Simple Plan

Most people walk into family gatherings hoping things will go well. Hope is not a plan.

A plan doesn't mean rehearsing speeches or anticipating every possible comment. It means knowing, in advance, what topics tend to trigger you, which people tend to push your buttons, what your early exit options are, and what you'll say when you don't want to engage. Even a loose plan keeps your nervous system calmer. You're less likely to overreact, overexplain, or stay longer than you should.

You don't need to control the room.
You just need to control your next move.

Chapter 3
Spotting Trouble Before It Starts

Most difficult moments at family gatherings don't come out of nowhere. They build quietly. A look. A familiar tone. A comment that seems harmless on the surface but carries a familiar edge.

By the time the conversation feels openly uncomfortable, you're often already reacting instead of choosing how to respond. This chapter is about recognizing the early signals, before things escalate, so you can stay grounded and in control.

The Early Warning Signs Are Usually Subtle

People often expect conflict to announce itself clearly.

Raised voices.
Harsh words.
Obvious disrespect.

In reality, most family tension starts much smaller.

It might sound like:

"I'm just worried about you."
"I didn't mean anything by it."
"You're too sensitive."
"I was only joking."

These phrases aren't always harmful on their own.

What matters is the pattern and the timing. If a comment reliably leaves you feeling tense, defensive, or on edge, that's information worth paying attention to, even if the words themselves sound polite.Your body often notices trouble before your mind does.

Pay Attention to Your First Internal Reaction

One of the most reliable indicators that a conversation is heading in the wrong direction is your own internal response. You might notice a tightness in your chest, a sudden urge to explain yourself, the impulse to defend or justify, or a spike of irritation or guilt.

These reactions don't mean you're overreacting. They mean you've encountered a familiar trigger. The mistake many people make is ignoring this moment and pushing through, hoping the conversation will improve on its own. It rarely does. Catching that first reaction gives you a chance to choose a different response before emotions take over.

Common Patterns That Signal Trouble

Certain behaviors tend to repeat themselves at family gatherings. Once you recognize them, they become much easier to manage. Some of the most common include:

The concern that feels like criticism
Comments framed as care that still feel diminishing or intrusive.

The joke that isn't really a joke
Humor that consistently lands at your expense.

The topic that never goes well
Money, parenting, relationships, career choices, or lifestyle decisions that reliably turn tense.

The boundary test
Someone pushing for details you've avoided sharing before.

The pile-on
A comment that invites others to weigh in, often under the guise of group concern.

None of these requires immediate confrontation. They do require awareness.

The Difference Between Discomfort and Danger

Not every uncomfortable moment needs intervention. Family gatherings involve different personalities, opinions, and habits. Mild awkwardness is often unavoidable. A helpful question to ask yourself is this: Does this situation feel uncomfortable, or does it feel familiar in a way that usually ends badly?

If you've seen the ending before, you don't need to replay the scene.

Awareness Is Not the Same as Overthinking

There's a difference between being alert and being on edge. Awareness means noticing what's happening without immediately acting on it. Overthinking means replaying every word and anticipating problems that may never come.

This chapter is not about hypervigilance. It's about recognizing familiar signals so you can respond calmly when they appear. That awareness creates space. And space gives you choices.

What Comes Next

Now that you know what to watch for, the next step is knowing what to do when those early signals appear.

In the next chapters, we'll move into clear, usable responses, starting with neutral language that helps shut things down without escalating tension or inviting debate.

☐ You don't need clever comebacks.

☐ You don't need emotional speeches.

☐ You need calm, simple options you can rely on.

Chapter 4
Decide Your Goal Before You Arrive

Most people attend family gatherings with a vague hope. They hope it will be fine. They hope no one says anything. They hope they can just get through it.

Hope feels comforting, but it leaves you unprepared. Walking into a difficult environment without a clear goal makes it much easier to get pulled into conversations, emotions, and dynamics you never intended to engage with.

This chapter is about deciding, in advance, what you want from the gathering and what you do not. That decision alone can change how the entire event unfolds.

Why Going in Without a Goal Makes Things Harder

When you do not decide your goal ahead of time, you tend to default to old patterns.

☐ You stay longer than you planned.

☐ You explain yourself more than you wanted to.

☐ You tolerate comments you promised yourself you would not.

This is not because you lack willpower. It is because decision-making is much harder when emotions are already activated. Once you feel tense, defensive, or guilty, your brain shifts into reaction mode. At that point, it is much harder to choose a calm, measured response. Deciding your goal beforehand reduces the number of decisions you have to make in the moment.

Your Goal Is Not to Fix Anything

This part is important.

Your goal for a family gathering does not need to be:

- ☐ Being understood
- ☐ Changing someone's opinion
- ☐ Resolving long-standing issues
- ☐ Having an honest conversation

Those goals often require time, privacy, emotional safety, and willingness from all sides. Family gatherings rarely provide those conditions. Trying to achieve them in that setting often leads to frustration and regret.

For this book, your goal should be much simpler. Your goal is to leave the gathering feeling intact.

Common Goals That Actually Work

Helpful goals are realistic, limited, and within your control.

Examples include:

- ☐ Staying for a specific amount of time
- ☐ Avoiding certain topics
- ☐ Keeping interactions polite and brief
- ☐ Not engaging in debates or defenses
- ☐ Leaving without an argument

These goals do not depend on anyone else's behavior. They depend on your choices. That makes them achievable.

Decide What You Are Willing to Engage In

Before you arrive, take a moment to think about what you are open to and what you are not.

You might decide:

☐ You are willing to make small talk but not discuss personal decisions

☐ You are willing to listen but not respond to criticism

☐ You are willing to be present but not stay past a certain point

This is not about rigidity. It is about clarity. When you know your limits ahead of time, it becomes much easier to recognize when a conversation is moving outside them.

Decide How Long You Are Staying

Time is one of the most effective boundaries you have, and one of the least confrontational. Deciding in advance how long you will stay gives you an automatic exit point. It prevents the slow drift from "this is manageable" to "I should have left an hour ago."

You do not need to announce your time limit. You only need to know it.

Decide What Success Looks Like

Success at a family gathering does not mean that everything went smoothly. It does not mean no one was difficult. It does not mean you felt comfortable the entire time.

Success means:

☐ You noticed when things started to shift

☐ You responded intentionally instead of reacting

☐ You protected your energy

☐ You left when it made sense

That is a reasonable standard.Anything beyond that is a bonus.

Write Your Plan Down, Even Briefly

A plan does not need to be detailed. It can be as simple as:

☐ I am staying for two hours.

☐ I am not discussing this topic.

☐ I will leave if the conversation turns personal.

Writing it down helps anchor it in your mind. It also gives you something to return to if you start second-guessing yourself during the event.

What Comes Next

Now that you know what you are walking into and what your goal is, the next step is knowing what to say when conversations begin to drift.

The following chapters focus on neutral, simple language you can use to shut things down without escalating tension or inviting debate.

☐ You do not need perfect words.

☐ You need a few reliable ones.

☐ That is where we go next.

Chapter 5
Neutral Responses That Shut Things Down

When family conversations turn uncomfortable, many people feel pressure to respond perfectly. To explain themselves clearly. To defend their choices. To correct misunderstandings.

That pressure often makes things worse. This chapter focuses on a different approach: neutral responses that reduce tension rather than escalate it. Neutral responses are not clever. They are not confrontational. They are not emotionally revealing. They are simple, steady, and effective.

Why Neutral Responses Work

Most difficult family comments are invitations.

- An invitation to explain.
- An invitation to argue.
- An invitation to defend yourself.

When you accept the invitation, the conversation expands. Neutral responses decline the invitation without making a point of it.

They do not challenge the other person.
They do not invest emotional energy in the comment.
They do not require agreement or approval.

They simply stop the momentum.

What Neutral Does Not Mean

Neutral does not mean cold.

It does not mean rude.

It does not mean passive.

It does not mean pretending you are unaffected.

Neutral means responding in a way that gives the conversation nowhere interesting to go. Think of it as closing a door quietly instead of slamming it.

Core Neutral Phrases You Can Rely On

These phrases work across many situations. They are intentionally unspecific.

You can adjust the wording to sound natural to you.

- ☐ "I've got it handled."
- ☐ "I'm comfortable with my decision."
- ☐ "That works for me."
- ☐ "I'm not worried about it."
- ☐ "I've thought about it."

Used calmly, these phrases signal that the topic is not open for discussion.

They do not invite follow-up.

When the Comment Is Framed as Concern

Comments framed as concern often sound reasonable on the surface.

They can be the hardest to respond to without feeling defensive.

Examples include:

- ☐ "I'm just worried about you."
- ☐ "I only want what's best for you."
- ☐ "Have you really thought this through?"

Neutral responses keep the tone polite while closing the conversation.

Try:

- ☐ "I appreciate the concern."
- ☐ "I've thought about it, thanks."
- ☐ "I'm comfortable with where things are."

You do not need to add explanations. Concern does not require compliance.

When the Comment Is a Subtle Dig

Subtle digs often come disguised as humor or observation.

They might sound like:

- ☐ "You're still doing that?"
- ☐ "Must be nice to have that kind of time."
- ☐ "Well, that's one way to do it."

These comments are designed to provoke a reaction. Neutral responses remove the payoff.

Try:

- ☐ "It works for me."
- ☐ "That's how I chose to handle it."
- ☐ "I'm okay with it."

Delivered calmly, these responses signal that the comment did not land.

When the Topic Is Personal or Invasive

Some questions cross a line without sounding aggressive.

They may involve money, relationships, health, parenting, or future plans.

You are not required to answer personal questions just because they were asked.

Neutral responses give you a way out without confrontation.

Try:

☐ "I'm keeping that private."

☐ "I'm not getting into that today."

☐ "I'd rather not discuss it here."

These statements are complete. You do not owe justification.

Let Silence Do Some of the Work

After a neutral response, pause. You do not need to fill the space. Silence often feels uncomfortable, but it is effective. Many people will change the subject on their own once they realize there is nothing more to extract. If they do not, you can repeat your response calmly or redirect the conversation.

Repetition Is Not Rudeness

If someone pushes after a neutral response, repeating yourself is appropriate.

Use the same words.
Use the same tone.
Do not add new information.

Repetition signals consistency, not hostility.

This is one of the most effective ways to avoid escalation.

What Comes Next

Neutral responses are your first line of defense. They work best early, before emotions rise.

In the next chapter, we will focus on what to do when neutral responses are ignored, and someone continues to push. You will learn how to hold your ground without raising the stakes or turning the moment into a confrontation. That is where things often feel hardest, and where the right language matters most.

Chapter 6
When They Push After You Respond

Neutral responses work well, but they do not always end the conversation. Some people push anyway.

They repeat the question.
They reframe the comment.
They insist on clarification.

This is often the moment when tension spikes, not because the comment itself is worse, but because the pressure increases. This chapter is about what to do next, without escalating the situation or abandoning your boundaries.

Why Pushing Is So Common

When someone pushes after you respond neutrally, it is usually not because they did not hear you. It is because they expected more.

More explanation.
More engagement.
More emotional access.

When they do not get it, they try again. Understanding this helps you avoid taking the push personally. It is not a failure of your response. It is a test of whether the boundary will hold.

The Power of Calm Repetition

One of the most effective responses to pushing is repetition. This does not mean restating your point more forcefully or with better arguments. It means repeating the same response, calmly and consistently.

For example:

☐ "I'm comfortable with my decision."

☐ "I've thought about it."

☐ "I'm not getting into that."

When repeated without added emotion or detail, these phrases lose their entertainment value. They give the other person nothing new to engage with.

What Makes Repetition Work

Repetition works because it changes the dynamic.

Instead of a debate, the interaction becomes predictable.

☐ You are not escalating.

☐ You are not withdrawing.

☐ You are simply holding your position.

Many people stop pushing once they realize the conversation is not going anywhere. Consistency is more important than wording.

Avoid the Urge to Clarify

When someone pushes, the natural impulse is to clarify.

To explain what you meant.
To soften your response.
To justify your choice.

Clarifying often reopens the conversation. It introduces new details that can be questioned or criticized. If your original response was clear and respectful, it does not need improvement. Silence or repetition is usually more effective than clarification.

Redirecting Without Deflecting

If repetition feels too blunt for the situation, redirection is another option. Redirection changes the subject without calling attention to the shift.

For example:

- ☐ "Anyway, did you try the food yet?"
- ☐ "How has work been going for you?"
- ☐ "I wanted to ask you about something else."

Redirection works best when delivered casually. You are not avoiding the topic. You are choosing a different one.

When Humor Helps, and When It Doesn't

Light humor can sometimes ease tension, but it should be used carefully. Helpful humor is brief and non-defensive.Unhelpful humor:

- ☐ Masks discomfort
- ☐ Turns into sarcasm
- ☐ Invites teasing or follow-up

If humor tends to backfire in your family, it is better to rely on neutral language instead. Calm and boring is often safer than clever.

Knowing When to Pause the Interaction

If pushing continues despite repetition or redirection, taking a short pause can help.This might mean:

- ☐ Stepping away to get a drink
- ☐ Using the restroom

☐ Joining another conversation

A pause breaks the momentum without requiring explanation. You are allowed to disengage temporarily.

When Holding Your Ground Feels Uncomfortable

Holding your ground may feel awkward at first.You might worry about seeming rude, cold, or difficult. That discomfort does not mean you are doing something wrong. It means you are changing a familiar pattern. Most people feel uneasy the first few times they do not give the expected response. That feeling usually passes.

What Comes Next

So far, we have focused on language that helps you avoid escalation.

In the next chapter, we will look at the opposite side of the problem, the things people often say in these moments that make situations worse, even when their intentions are good. Knowing what not to say can be just as important as knowing what to say. That is where we go next.

Chapter 7
What Not to Say (Even Though You Want To)

There are moments at family gatherings when the urge to speak feels overwhelming.

You want to correct the record.
You want to explain yourself.
You want to say the thing you have been holding in for years.

Most people get into trouble not because they lack the right words, but because they use the wrong ones at the wrong time. This chapter is about recognizing those moments and choosing restraint instead.

The Trap of Overexplaining

Overexplaining often starts with good intentions.

- ☐ You want to be understood.
- ☐ You want to prevent assumptions.
- ☐ You want your choices make sense to others.

Unfortunately, overexplaining usually invites more questions, more opinions, and more judgment. Each additional detail creates another opening. Instead of closing the conversation, it expands it. A short response may feel insufficient, but it is often more effective than a detailed one. Clarity does not require completeness.

Why Defending Yourself Backfires

Defending yourself feels logical when you sense criticism.

- ☐ You list your reasons.
- ☐ You explain your process.
- ☐ You point out the effort you have made.

In emotionally charged family settings, defense is often interpreted as a sign of uncertainty. It signals that the topic is still open. The more you defend, the more others feel entitled to weigh in. Not every comment deserves a rebuttal. Sometimes the strongest response is a calm, unelaborated statement of where you stand.

Emotional Honesty at the Wrong Time

There is a time and place for emotional honesty. A crowded family gathering is rarely it. Sharing vulnerable feelings in a tense, public setting often leads to misunderstanding, minimization, or unintended escalation.

You may be met with:

- ☐ Advice you did not ask for
- ☐ Jokes meant to lighten the mood
- ☐ Defensiveness from others

That response can leave you feeling exposed instead of supported. Emotional honesty is not wrong. It is just context-dependent. This book focuses on helping you get through events intact, not processing everything in real time.

The Temptation to Settle Old Scores

Family gatherings can stir up memories.

- ☐ Old grievances.
- ☐ Past slights.
- ☐ Conversations that never happened.

When emotions rise, it can feel like the perfect moment to finally address them. It rarely is.Group settings, time pressure, and heightened emotions make productive resolution unlikely. Bringing up the past often shifts the focus away from the present moment and into defensiveness or denial. That usually creates more distance, not less.

Sarcasm and Passive Remarks

Sarcasm can feel satisfying in the moment. It can also escalate tension quickly. Passive remarks often land harder than intended, especially in families where history already exists. Even when others are being indirect, responding in kind often worsens the situation. If sarcasm has ever come back to haunt you later, that is a sign to avoid it here. Calm and direct language is usually safer.

Explaining Your Boundaries Repeatedly

You may feel tempted to explain your boundaries in detail, especially if someone questions them. Long explanations often invite debate. They also give others the impression that your boundary is negotiable. A boundary does not need to be persuasive. It only needs to be clear. Repeating a simple statement is usually more effective than expanding on it.

Letting Guilt Drive Your Words

Guilt is one of the most powerful forces at family gatherings.

- ☐ It can push you to say yes when you mean no.
- ☐ It can push you to explain when you wanted to stop talking.
- ☐ It can push you to stay longer than you planned.

Words spoken out of guilt often lead to regret. Pausing before responding gives you a chance to choose words that align with your plan, not your discomfort.

When Saying Less Is the Better Choice

Silence is often underestimated.

- ☐ Not every comment needs a response.
- ☐ Not every question needs an answer.
- ☐ Not every moment needs to be filled.

Choosing not to engage can feel uncomfortable, especially if you are used to smoothing things over. That discomfort usually fades faster than the regret of saying too much.

What Comes Next

Knowing what not to say helps you avoid common pitfalls. In the next chapter, we will focus on situations where the tension is public, when comments are made in front of others, and the pressure to respond feels higher. You will learn how to handle group dynamics without becoming the villain or the topic of conversation. That is where we go next.

Chapter 8
Handling Group Situations Without Becoming the Villain

One-on-one conversations are easier to manage. Group situations are different. When comments are made in front of others, the pressure to respond increases. You may feel watched, judged, or silently evaluated. Even neutral moments can suddenly feel like performances. This is often where people say things they later regret, not because they wanted conflict, but because they felt cornered. This chapter is about staying steady when the audience changes the dynamic.

Why Group Settings Raise the Stakes

Group settings amplify everything. A comment that might feel manageable in private can feel humiliating or aggressive in front of others. Silence can feel like agreement. A response can feel like a challenge. People may jump in with opinions, jokes, or advice, even if they were not involved moments earlier. Once a group becomes engaged, the situation can escalate quickly.

Understanding this helps you respond more strategically.

The Myth That You Need to Correct the Narrative

When something uncomfortable is said publicly, many people feel an immediate urge to set the record straight.

- □ To clarify.
- □ To defend themselves.
- □ To make sure others do not get the wrong idea.

This urge is understandable, but it often backfires. Trying to manage how everyone perceives you can pull you into long explanations or public debates that leave you feeling exposed. You are not required to manage the room. You are only responsible for your own behavior.

Use Short Responses That Do Not Invite Commentary

In group settings, brevity is your ally. Short responses reduce the likelihood of follow-up questions or commentary from others.

Examples include:

- □ "I'm comfortable with my choice."
- □ "That works for me."
- □ "I've got it handled."

Delivered calmly, these responses signal that the topic is closed. They do not invite discussion or approval.

Avoid Turning to the Group for Support

It can be tempting to look for allies in the room.

- □ To make eye contact.
- □ To laugh nervously.
- □ To seek validation from others.

This can unintentionally turn the moment into a group event. It also increases the chance that someone else will jump in, often in ways that make things worse. Keeping your response directed to the original speaker helps keep the interaction contained.

When Others Pile On

Sometimes a comment opens the door for others to join in.

Advice starts flying.
Opinions multiply.
The conversation drifts further away from what you want to discuss.

This is a good moment to disengage.

You might say:

- □ "I'm not getting into this right now."
- □ "Let's change the subject."
- □ "I'm going to step away for a bit."

You do not need a consensus to disengage.

Exiting a Group Conversation Gracefully

Leaving a group conversation does not need to be dramatic. Simple transitions often work best:

- □ Excusing yourself to get a drink
- □ Helping in another room
- □ Joining a different conversation
- □ Stepping outside briefly

These exits shift attention away from you and give the moment time to cool down. You do not owe an explanation for moving on.

When Someone Tries to Make You the Problem

In group settings, boundary-setting can sometimes be reframed as rudeness or overreaction.

Comments like:

☐ "We're just talking."

☐ "You don't have to be so sensitive."

☐ "No one else minds."

These statements are designed to pressure you into compliance.

A calm response might be:

☐ "I'm okay stepping away."

☐ "I'm just choosing not to engage."

☐ "I'm going to leave it there."

You are allowed to remove yourself from conversations that do not feel respectful.

Staying Out of the After-Conversation Gossip

What happens after a group interaction can matter just as much as the moment itself. Resist the urge to explain yourself privately to others afterward. Post-event explanations often reopen the situation and keep it alive longer than necessary. If asked about it later, a neutral response is enough:

☐ "I just needed a break."

☐ "It wasn't a big deal."

Letting the moment pass without commentary often prevents it from becoming a story.

What Comes Next

So far, we have focused on language and behavior that help you navigate conversations as they happen. In the next section of the book, we will shift from talking to doing.

We will focus on emotional containment, quiet boundaries, and managing what happens inside you during and after these gatherings. These skills help you leave feeling steadier, even when the situation itself is imperfect. That is where we go next.

Chapter 9
Emotional Containment (Without Shutting Down)

E ven when you say the right things, family gatherings can still stir up strong emotions.

☐ You may feel tense.

☐ You may feel irritated.

☐ You may feel suddenly small, angry, or overwhelmed.

Emotional containment is not about suppressing those feelings or pretending they do not exist. It is about keeping them from running the show. This chapter is about staying present and steady, without shutting down or losing yourself in the moment.

What Emotional Containment Actually Means

Emotional containment means allowing emotions to exist without acting on them immediately. It is the ability to notice what you are feeling, acknowledge it internally, and choose your response rather than react automatically. Containment is not numbness. It is not denial. It is not pretending everything is fine. It is a skill that lets you stay functional in difficult environments.

Why Family Settings Make Emotions Stronger

Family gatherings often lower your emotional defenses.

☐ Old roles resurface.

☐ Familiar voices trigger familiar reactions.

☐ Unresolved history sits just beneath the surface.

Your nervous system recognizes the environment, even if you have changed. That is why reactions can feel sudden or disproportionate. Understanding this helps reduce self-judgment. You are not weak. You are responding to a charged setting.

Notice the Physical Signals First

Emotions usually show up in the body before they form into thoughts.

You might notice:

- ☐ Tight shoulders or jaw
- ☐ A racing heart
- ☐ Shallow breathing
- ☐ A sudden urge to escape or speak quickly

These signals are early warnings. Noticing them gives you a moment to pause before reacting. A brief internal check can help: What am I feeling right now? Where do I feel it?

You do not need to analyze the answer. Just noticing is enough.

Slow the Moment Down

When emotions rise, everything can feel urgent. Slowing the moment down gives you space. Simple ways to do this include:

- ☐ Taking a slow breath before responding
- ☐ Putting your feet flat on the ground
- ☐ Taking a sip of water
- ☐ Letting a second of silence pass before speaking

These small actions help regulate your nervous system without drawing attention.

You Do Not Have to Match the Energy in the Room

When others are agitated, emotional, or provocative, it can feel natural to meet them at that level. You do not have to. Matching someone else's energy often escalates situations. Lowering your energy can stabilize them, or at least keep you steady. Calm responses can feel unnatural at first, especially if you are used to explaining or defending yourself. With practice, they become easier.

Stay Present Without Engaging Internally

You can be present in a conversation without engaging emotionally. This might look like:

☐ Listening without preparing a response

☐ Letting comments pass without internal debate

☐ Reminding yourself that you do not need to resolve anything right now

Presence does not require participation. You are allowed to observe rather than absorb.

Give Yourself Permission to Step Away

Emotional containment does not mean staying in situations that are overwhelming. Stepping away briefly is often a wise choice. This might mean:

☐ Taking a short walk

☐ Using the restroom

☐ Spending a few minutes outside

☐ Shifting to a quieter space

These breaks help reset your nervous system and prevent emotional overload. You do not need to justify taking space.

After the Moment Passes

Once the intensity fades, you may notice lingering thoughts or emotions.That is normal. Resist the urge to immediately evaluate how you did. You can reflect later, when you are calmer.

In the moment, your goal is simple.

☐ Stay steady.

☐ Protect your energy.

☐ Get through the event intact.

What Comes Next

Emotional containment helps you manage what happens inside you. In the next chapter, we will focus on boundaries, how to maintain them quietly and consistently without turning them into announcements or confrontations. These boundaries work alongside emotional containment to keep situations from escalating. That is where we go next.

Chapter 10
Boundaries That Don't Trigger a Scene

When people hear the word boundaries, they often imagine confrontation.

☐ Clear statements.

☐ Firm tones.

☐ Strong reactions.

That image alone can make boundaries feel risky, especially at family gatherings where emotions are already close to the surface.This chapter focuses on a quieter approach.

☐ Boundaries that are effective without being dramatic.

☐ Boundaries that protect you without demanding agreement.

☐ Boundaries that work even when others do not like them.

What a Boundary Actually Is

A boundary is not a rule for someone else. It is a limit on what you will engage with, tolerate, or participate in. That distinction matters.

When boundaries are framed as attempts to control others, they often fail. When they are framed as decisions about your own behavior, they tend to hold.

☐ You cannot make someone stop talking.

☐ You can decide not to participate in the conversation.

☐ You cannot make someone respect your choices.

☐ You can decide how much access they have to you.

Quiet Boundaries Are Often the Strongest

Loud boundaries draw attention. Quiet boundaries create consistency. Quiet boundaries look like:

- ☐ Changing the subject without explanation
- ☐ Giving brief responses instead of full answers
- ☐ Leaving earlier than planned
- ☐ Stepping away when conversations cross a line

These actions do not announce anything. They simply shift your participation. Over time, they often reduce the need for repeated pressure.

Why Announcing Boundaries Backfires

Announcing a boundary can feel empowering. It can also invite debate. Statements that often trigger defensiveness, especially in family settings:

- ☐ "I won't tolerate this."
- ☐ "You need to respect my boundaries."
- ☐ "I'm setting a boundary."

They turn the moment into a discussion about fairness, intent, or tone. This book emphasizes boundaries that function without requiring understanding or approval. You do not need permission to protect your peace.

Decide Your Non-Negotiables in Advance

Boundaries are easier to maintain when you decide them before emotions are involved. Ask yourself:

- ☐ What topics am I not willing to discuss?

- How long am I willing to stay?
- What behavior will cause me to disengage?

These decisions do not need to be shared. They just need to be clear to you.

Boundaries Are Maintained Through Action

A boundary only works if it is followed by action. For example:

- If you decide not to discuss a topic, change the subject, or disengage when it comes up.
- If you decide to leave when things escalate, follow through.
- If you decide to keep responses brief, resist the urge to explain later.

Action reinforces the boundary more than words ever will.

When Others Push Against Your Boundary

It is common for people to test boundaries, especially if they are new.

- They may question you.
- They may minimize your response.
- They may act surprised.

This does not mean the boundary is wrong.It means it is unfamiliar. Calm repetition and consistent action are usually enough. You do not need to convince anyone.

Managing the Discomfort That Comes With Boundaries

Holding boundaries can feel uncomfortable, especially if you are used to accommodating others. You might feel:

- Guilty

☐ Self-conscious

☐ Concerned about how you are perceived

These feelings do not mean you should abandon the boundary. They mean you are doing something different. Discomfort often fades with repetition. Regret tends to last longer.

Boundaries Can Be Adjusted

Boundaries are not permanent declarations. They can change based on circumstances, relationships, and your capacity. What matters is that they are intentional. You are allowed to decide, gathering by gathering, what works for you.

What Comes Next

So far, we have focused on staying steady, responding neutrally, and maintaining quiet boundaries. The next chapter will address something just as important: what happens after the gathering is over. Managing the aftermath inside your own head can determine whether the experience lingers or fades. That is where we go next.

Chapter 11
Managing the Aftermath Inside Your Head

For many people, the hardest part of a family gathering comes after it ends.

☐ You replay conversations.

☐ You rethink your responses.

☐ You wonder if you were too quiet, too firm, or not firm enough.

Even if the gathering went reasonably well, your mind may keep returning to it. This chapter is about what to do after the event, so it does not take up more space than it deserves.

Why the Aftermath Can Feel Worse Than the Event

During the gathering, you are focused on getting through it. Afterward, the pressure drops. That is often when emotions surface. Your nervous system begins to unwind, and your mind looks for meaning, mistakes, or unfinished business. This can lead to rumination, second-guessing, and guilt. This response is common. It does not mean you handled things poorly. It means you were in a stressful environment and are now coming down from it.

Resist the Urge to Grade Yourself

Many people mentally score their performance after a gathering.

☐ What they should have said.

☐ What they should not have said.

☐ What they wish they had done differently.

This habit is rarely helpful. Grading yourself keeps the event alive longer than necessary and reinforces unrealistic standards. Instead, ask yourself one simple question. Did I protect my peace reasonably well? That is the only metric that matters here.

Separate Discomfort From Failure

Not all discomfort is a sign of failure. You can feel uncomfortable and still have handled the situation well. You can leave feeling unsettled and still have honored your boundaries. Discomfort often comes from breaking old patterns, not from doing something wrong. Remind yourself of this distinction when doubt creeps in.

Watch for Guilt-Based Thinking

Guilt often shows up after family gatherings. You might think:

- ☐ I should have stayed longer.
- ☐ I should have explained myself.
- ☐ I should not have made things awkward.

These thoughts tend to assume responsibility for other people's feelings. That responsibility is rarely yours.

- ☐ You are allowed to leave when you need to.
- ☐ You are allowed to keep things private.
- ☐ You are allowed to disengage.

Feeling guilty does not mean you made a mistake.

Do Not Reopen the Event Unnecessarily

After a gathering, it can be tempting to revisit what happened.

- ☐ To send follow-up messages.
- ☐ To explain your behavior.
- ☐ To smooth things over.

Unless something truly requires clarification, reopening the event often creates more tension, not less. Letting things settle quietly is usually the better choice. Not every moment needs closure.

Ground Yourself in the Present

One of the most effective ways to stop rumination is to reconnect with the present moment. This might include:

- ☐ Going for a walk
- ☐ Taking a shower
- ☐ Eating a meal
- ☐ Watching or reading something familiar
- ☐ Getting rest

These simple actions signal to your nervous system that the situation has passed. You are no longer in the room.

Take Note of What Worked

When you feel ready, reflect briefly on what went well. This is not about perfection.

It might be:

- ☐ You noticed tension earlier than usual.
- ☐ You stayed calmer than you expected.
- ☐ You left before things escalated.
- ☐ You said less instead of more.

These small successes matter. They build confidence for future gatherings.

Let the Experience End

The gathering does not need to follow you home. You are allowed to put it down.

Remind yourself:

- ☐ I did the best I could with what I had.
- ☐ I do not need to keep thinking about this. I can move on now.

Sometimes the healthiest response is simply to let the moment end.

What Comes Next

Managing the aftermath helps prevent one gathering from coloring the next.

In the final chapters, we will focus on recognizing when staying is no longer helpful and how to leave without creating additional conflict. Knowing when to go and how to do it calmly can change everything. That is where we go next.

Chapter 12
How to Know When It's Time to Go

Knowing when to leave a family gathering can be harder than knowing how to respond. Many people stay longer than they want to because they feel obligated, worried about appearances, or unsure whether their discomfort is "enough" to justify leaving. This chapter is about recognizing when staying is no longer helpful and trusting yourself to act on that information.

You Do Not Need a Dramatic Reason to Leave

Many people believe they need a clear incident to justify leaving.

- ☐ A raised voice.
- ☐ An argument.
- ☐ An obvious conflict.

In reality, most situations do not end with a clear breaking point. More often, there is a gradual shift.

- ☐ Your energy drops.
- ☐ Your patience thins.
- ☐ Your body feels tense or exhausted.

That is reason enough. You do not need permission to leave a situation that is no longer serving you.

Common Signs It Is Time to Go

Some signals are internal rather than external. You may notice:

- You are replaying the same conversation internally
- You feel emotionally flooded or shut down
- You are staying only to avoid guilt
- You are no longer present, just enduring

These signs matter. They indicate that your capacity has been reached. Leaving at this point can prevent regret later.

Staying Longer Rarely Improves Things

Many people stay because they hope things will improve.

- They wait for the conversation to shift.
- They hope someone will change the subject.
- They assume the moment will pass.

Sometimes it does. Often, it does not. Staying past your limit usually leads to sharper responses, increased resentment, or emotional exhaustion. Leaving earlier is often the kinder choice, for yourself and for others.

Trusting Your Internal Signals

Your body often knows before your mind does. Pay attention to:

- A tight chest
- A headache
- A sudden fatigue
- An urge to withdraw or escape

These are not signs of weakness. They are signals that your nervous system is overwhelmed. Honoring them is a form of self-respect.

The Difference Between Avoidance and Self-Protection

Leaving is sometimes framed as avoidance. In reality, there is a difference between avoiding discomfort and protecting your well-being. Avoidance is driven by fear. Self-protection is driven by awareness. Choosing to leave when a situation is no longer healthy is not avoidance. It is a measured response to a difficult environment.

You Do Not Have to Wait for Permission

You may feel pressure to stay because others expect it. You may worry about disappointing someone. You may fear being seen as rude or dramatic.

Those concerns are understandable. They are not obligations. You are allowed to prioritize your emotional safety, even if others would prefer you to stay.

Leaving Is a Skill

Like everything else in this book, leaving gets easier with practice. The first few times may feel awkward. You may question yourself afterward. That does not mean you made the wrong choice. It means you are learning to respond differently than you used to. Over time, your confidence will grow.

What Comes Next

Knowing when to leave is only half the equation. In the final chapter, we will focus on how to leave calmly and cleanly, without guilt, drama, or long explanations. That final piece helps ensure that leaving does not become another source of stress. That is where we go next.

Chapter 13
Leaving Without Drama, Guilt, or Explanations

L eaving a family gathering is often the moment people dread most. Not because they do not know how to leave physically, but because of what they expect to follow.

☐ Questions.

☐ Judgment.

☐ Disapproval.

This chapter is about leaving in a way that protects your peace, without turning the exit into a negotiation or a statement.

You Do Not Owe a Detailed Explanation

One of the biggest sources of stress around leaving is the belief that you owe people a full explanation. You do not.

Explanations often invite:

☐ Debate

☐ Persuasion

☐ Minimization

☐ Guilt

The more you explain, the more room there is for pushback. A simple reason is enough. Sometimes, no reason at all is better.

Keep Your Exit Language Brief

Short exits are usually the cleanest. They give the moment less weight and make it easier for others to move on. Examples include:

- ☐ "I'm going to head out."
- ☐ "I need to get going."
- ☐ "I'm going to call it a night."

These statements are complete. They do not require justification.

If You Feel Pressure to Explain

If someone presses for a reason, you can repeat a neutral explanation without adding detail.

Examples include:

- ☐ "I've got an early day tomorrow."
- ☐ "I'm ready to head home."
- ☐ "I'm feeling done for the day."

You are not required to make your reason convincing. You only need to state it calmly.

Avoid Apologizing for Leaving

Many people instinctively apologize when they leave.

"I'm sorry, I just need to go."

Apologies can unintentionally signal that you are doing something wrong.

You are not. Leaving when you need to is a reasonable choice. If you want to soften the exit without apologizing, gratitude can be more effective. For example:

- ☐ "Thanks for having me."
- ☐ "It was good to see everyone."

Do Not Announce Your Emotions on the Way Out

It can be tempting to explain how you feel as you leave.

- ☐ To clarify.
- ☐ To be honest.
- ☐ To make sure others understand.

Exit moments are rarely the right time for emotional conversations. Sharing feelings at that point often escalates the situation and keeps you emotionally engaged longer than you want to be. Leaving calmly allows the moment to end.

Expect Some Discomfort, and Let It Pass

Leaving may feel uncomfortable, even when it is the right choice. You might feel:

- ☐ Self-conscious
- ☐ Guilty
- ☐ Concerned about how you are perceived

These feelings are common when you change a familiar pattern. They usually fade more quickly than the regret of staying too long. Discomfort does not mean you made a mistake.

Leaving Is Not a Statement

One of the most helpful reframes is this. Leaving is not a message. It does not have to mean:

- [ ] You are angry
- [ ] You are upset
- [ ] You are cutting anyone off
- [ ] You are making a point

Sometimes it simply means you are done for the day. Allow your exit to be ordinary.

After You Leave

Once you are gone, resist the urge to replay the exit. You do not need to follow up with explanations or reassurance unless you genuinely want to. Let the moment settle. You can always address things later, in a more appropriate setting, if needed. Often, nothing more is required.

Bringing It All Together

This book has focused on practical skills you can use before, during, and after family gatherings. You learned how to:

- [ ] Recognize patterns early
- [ ] Decide your goal in advance
- [ ] Respond neutrally
- [ ] Hold quiet boundaries
- [ ] Manage emotional reactions
- [ ] Know when to leave

☐ Leave without escalating tension

None of this requires perfection. It requires awareness and practice. Each gathering is an opportunity to do a little better than last time.

A Final Thought

Family dynamics are complicated. You did not create them, and you cannot control them.

What you can control is how much space they take up in your life.

☐ You are allowed to protect your energy.

☐ You are allowed to leave when you need to. You are allowed to choose calm over conflict.

That choice matters.

And it is enough.

NOTE: A condensed version of everything in this book appears in the Quick Reference section that follows. You can return to it anytime you need a reminder.

Quick Reference
For Difficult Family Gatherings

This section is designed for quick use. You can skim it before a gathering, refer to it during a break, or revisit it afterward if your thoughts feel unsettled.

Use what applies. Ignore what doesn't.

Before You Go

Set Your Plan

Ask yourself:

- Why am I going?
- How long am I staying?
- What topics am I not engaging in?
- What will tell me it's time to leave?

Decide:

- A realistic arrival time
- A realistic departure time
- One or two neutral phrases you can rely on
- Your early exit option

You do not need to share this plan with anyone.

Early Warning Signs

Notice Before Things Escalate

Pay attention to:

- Tightness in your chest or jaw
- A sudden urge to explain yourself
- Familiar irritation or guilt
- Thoughts like "Here we go again."

These signals matter.

They mean it's time to slow down and respond intentionally.

Neutral Responses

Use These to Shut Things Down Calmly

These phrases work best when delivered evenly and without explanation.

- "I've got it handled."
- "I'm comfortable with my decision."
- "That works for me."
- "I'm not worried about it."
- "I'm not getting into that."

Repeat if necessary. Silence is also an option.

When Concern Is Used as Pressure

Try:

- "I appreciate the concern."
- "I've thought about it."
- "I'm okay with where things are."

Concern does not require compliance.

When the Comment Is a Subtle Dig

Try:

- ☐ "It works for me."
- ☐ "That's how I chose to handle it."
- ☐ "I'm fine with it."

Do not explain.
Do not justify.

What to Avoid Saying

Even If You Want To

Avoid:

- ☐ Overexplaining your choices
- ☐ Defending yourself
- ☐ Sharing vulnerable feelings in public
- ☐ Bringing up old grievances
- ☐ Using sarcasm
- ☐ Announcing boundaries

Saying less often protects you more.

Group Situations

Keep It Contained

Use short responses:

- ☐ "I've got it handled."
- ☐ "I'm okay with my choice."

Avoid:

- ☐ Looking to the group for validation
- ☐ Correcting the narrative publicly
- ☐ Explaining yourself afterward

If the group piles on, disengage.

Emotional Containment

Stay Present Without Absorbing Everything

Try:

- ☐ Slowing your breathing
- ☐ Placing your feet flat on the ground
- ☐ Taking a sip of water
- ☐ Letting a pause happen before speaking

You do not need to match the energy in the room.

Quiet Boundaries

Protect Your Peace Without Announcements

Boundaries can look like:

- ☐ Changing the subject
- ☐ Giving shorter responses
- ☐ Stepping away briefly
- ☐ Leaving earlier than planned

Boundaries are maintained through action, not explanation.

Signs It's Time to Leave

You may notice:

- ☐ Emotional exhaustion
- ☐ Replaying conversations internally
- ☐ Staying only to avoid guilt
- ☐ Feeling shut down or flooded

You do not need a dramatic reason to go.

Leaving Cleanly

Without Drama or Guilt

Use simple exits:

- ☐ "I'm going to head out."
- ☐ "I need to get going."
- ☐ "I'm calling it a night."

If pressed:

- ☐ "I'm ready to head home."
- ☐ "I'm done for the day."

Avoid apologizing.
Gratitude works better than explanations.

After the Gathering

Let It End

Remind yourself:

- ☐ I did the best I could.

□ I protected my peace.

□ I do not need to replay this.

Avoid reopening the event unless absolutely necessary.

Ground yourself in the present.

Keep This in Mind

□ You don't need perfect outcomes.

□ You don't need approval.

□ You don't need to explain yourself.

You just need a better plan.

And now you have one.

Conclusion
You're Not Difficult, This Is Difficult

Family gatherings can bring out parts of us we thought we had outgrown.

- ☐ Old dynamics resurface.
- ☐ Old expectations reappear.
- ☐ Old reactions try to take over.

If navigating these moments feels harder than it should, that does not mean you are failing. It means you are dealing with something complex.

This book was never about fixing your family or transforming every interaction. It was about giving you practical tools so these gatherings do not take more from you than they deserve. You learned how to notice patterns early, decide your goal before you arrive, respond neutrally, hold quiet boundaries, manage emotional reactions, and leave when it is time, without guilt or drama.

None of these skills requires perfection. They work best when applied gradually, imperfectly, and with self-compassion.

- ☐ Some gatherings will still feel awkward.
- ☐ Some moments will still sting.
- ☐ Some people will still be difficult.

That does not erase your progress.

- ☐ Every time you pause instead of reacting, you are changing the pattern.
- ☐ Every time you say less instead of more, you are protecting your energy.
- ☐ Every time you leave when you need to, you are honoring yourself.

Those small choices add up.

You may not notice the shift immediately, but over time, these gatherings will begin to feel more manageable. Shorter. Lighter. Less consuming.

Most importantly, they will stop defining who you are.

- ☐ You are allowed to show up without overexplaining.
- ☐ You are allowed to disengage without making a point.
- ☐ You are allowed to leave without apologizing.

You are not asking for too much. You are asking for reasonable peace in an unreasonable situation. That is not selfish.It is necessary. Carry what works from this book with you. Leave the rest behind. Return to it when you need a reminder that you are not alone in this and that you are capable of handling it calmly, on your own terms.

That is enough.

The Toxic Family Series

If this book resonated with you, the following titles explore related patterns in greater depth. Each book stands on its own and can be read in any order.

☐ **Toxic Family Gatherings**
What to Say, How to Act, and When to Leave Without Making Things Worse

☐ **Toxic Family Roles**
How to Recognize the Patterns, Stop Carrying What Isn't Yours, and Reclaim Your Place

☐ **Toxic Family Conversations**
How to Spot Manipulation, Defuse Guilt, and End Conversations That Go Nowhere

☐ **Toxic Family Boundaries**
Setting Limits Without Over-Explaining and Holding Them When Others Push Back

About The Author

The author of the *Toxic Family Series* writes practical, non-diagnostic guidance for people navigating difficult family dynamics.

These books are not meant to label, analyze, or assign blame. They are designed to offer clarity, language, and options for disengaging from harmful patterns without escalating conflict.

The focus is not on who the author is, but on what helps. Each book stands on its own and is intended to be used quietly, thoughtfully, and at the reader's discretion.